Booze House

Snap Shot Stories

by Maria Mendoza

Booze House

authored by
Maria Mendoza

published by
William Joseph K Publications
PO BOX
Royal Oak MI 48067
www.williamjkpub.com

ISBN: 978-0-9820425-4-0
LCCN: 2009931450
Printed in the United States

Acknowledgement

To my husband Matthew for his love and support, and for always believing in me.

Introduction

For whatever reasons, there are people who choose to live lives filled with vice, surrounded by strife, and without an apprehension of consequence. The 'Live hard, die young' motto was one my Mother adopted long before I was born. It was never a life I wanted to be a part of, but I was. This is my story.

Maria Mendoza

Contents

Witchy Woman

Mom, forty-three with sags and bags seen through near sheer spandex and miniskirts, her dark straight hair sprouting gray wings from side to side, skin tinted a brown natural tan even in Michigan's coldest winter months. I never knew a day she wasn't strong, in charge, and oozing with confidence.

Mom enjoyed hot days spent in our backyard drinking mixes of vodka and grapefruit juice, nights dancing alone in a dark candle lit house blasting Def Leopard or sometimes even Eminem. Her seductive moves spinning remnants of days that once paid her to dance in the nude. Welfare didn't cover all the cost of having four kids, and minimum wage paying jobs were a joke. Mom, always clever, never failed at finding ways to get us by in life.

Things could have been different, a bit more peaceful, if it weren't for the drinking and the drugs, but at least the latter kept her at home and cool. The booze always stirred up anger and resentment, the crack, her illegal antidepressant.

Jack Daniels was to blame that night, intoxicating her early on. It was a cool October in '99, the night before Halloween. She hadn't had a driver's license because of her drinking in years, normally cabed it, or had me drop her off at the bar, but she decided to be her own chauffeur this time. Set her face with sparkles and dark eyeliner, a short skirt with a tight knit to wear, no disguise for her tonight. She didn't hurt no one but herself, cop caught her, didn't even make it very far.

Now at twenty-one, Mom and me frequented many of the same bars and nightclubs. Our paths may have even crossed that night, Mom leaving Clovers just minutes before *my* arrival. My attire fit the night. I wore a black sleek polyester dress with

long belled out sleeves. I lacked the pointed hat, but topped
the outfit off by allowing my naturally witchy hair to run wild,
painting in a single dark mole on my cheekbone. The dress
flattered my skinny pale bod, but pushed my tiny tits into a
more flattened state.

I was still with Brian that night. I had broken up with him
months before, just hadn't clued *him* in yet. My choices in men,
poor to say the least, always dysfunctional in a drug or drunken
way, and this one held a commonality with my Mother's drunk
driving history. I never allowed myself to get too attached.
Always hurt boys before they could hurt me. Learned that from
the one that took my virginity away at just fifteen.

The costume contest began, the stage rough and ready,
contestants crammed along the strung lit dark paneled walls,
tables shifted to create the catwalk for judging who could be
the best in creative costume dress. I didn't dare try to compete,
didn't have my booze boosting confidence in me that night.

'Hit me Baby one more time' played like clockwork down the
line. With each turn the Britney Spears impersonators
reenacted moves from the video, swinging their plaid miniskirts
to the sky, launching howls from the crowd of mostly men. I
had my fill. The drinks weren't going down smooth anyway.
Ditched the goodbyes and went on home to take care of my
little brother Joe. BillyJoe, or Joe for short, was always there.

I just moved back home for the third time. We lived in an
oversized white bungalow on a corner lot in the downriver city
of Wyandotte. It wasn't much.

Kevin took on the duty of watching BillyJoe that night in exchange for a joint, small fee, and a free dinner. He lied sprawled out on the overpriced off-white tweed Art Van living room couch I brought back home with me to replace Mom's broken down furniture. The left over pizza, brimming ashtray of cigarette butts, and a roach with a few hits left for his morning toke lied out on my wooden coffee table. It was the same recliner, couch, and table set I had when I lived with him.

Kevin, a year younger than me got too stuck on his drugs, tended to turn a bit abusive when he was without them. His six foot four overgrown figure was more than fearsome when in his pissed states, hence the *ex*, but also silly and dog cuddly, explaining our on again off again three year relationship. BillyJoe loved him anyway, so I let the past of our rocky relationship go and we remained friends.

Mom overtook mine and Carrie's shared bedroom on the second floor, Joe shifted into her old room at the foot of the stairs. His bed an oversized futon, allowing for me to comfortably crash out with him that night.

Shortly after, I was awoken by the ringing phone at 3:00 a.m., the operator announced "collect call from a Debbie Adams, will you accept the charges?" I sighed, accepting, scolding her for taking the car before she could get out a word on the dollar amount to pay for bail and to pick her up from the Southgate drunk tank.

She had been without a license for nearly six years due to previous charges, and was eligible to get her license back early next year. I hung up on her, then on to calling my Grandpa to go bail her out. She was his fuck up child not mine! Threw the phone and went back on to bed with Joe.

I woke up to sweet morning sounds of BillyJoe's feet wiggling back and forth against the bed sheets, muffled giggles and words from under the pillow "Sissy, Sissy, Sissy," one of the few words he often said. I giggled back giving him kisses on his cheek under the pillow.

At seventeen, BillyJoe towered at six feet tall, hair thick brown with waves, but it bothered him to keep long, so we kept it clipper short. He didn't understand his strength, sometimes he hit me too hard, stubborn, didn't like to be touched, and incapable of identifying with the world's demands, he could never be left unattended, we all catered to his needs and wants, wouldn't listen to many, but always recognized me as one of the few in charge.

For a first we prepared for what was to come. She was facing her third felony. She made a deal pleading guilty to welfare fraud at the age of nineteen. She wasn't aware of the welfare checks arriving at her parent's house down on Bruckner Street, and didn't want to admit who was cashing the checks during her employment at Fisher Bodies in Detroit. The second drunk driving offense came when I was fifteen, we stayed at my grandparent's house on Detroit's west side while she spent time in the Wayne County facility.

Without question caring for BillyJoe and keeping up the house was rolled out to me. I never denied my responsibility to care for him. A monthly supply of government money in the name of BillyJoe would keep us afloat until she returned, but Mom's repeated offenses left me fearing the worst this time around. I hoped the courts would be lenient, hoped they would understand BillyJoe *needed her* at home. I hoped, I hoped, I hoped.

That day in court, the female prosecutor unmerciful, Mom had given the 'feel sorry for me speech' about Joe one too many times. This being her third time in front of the same judge, the tears didn't matter. "You would have been there for your son's needs if you had been so concerned Mrs. Adams" came from the forty something black matriarch on the bench, who then went into her personal experience of caring for her own disabled daughter. She wasn't hearin' anymore of Mom's shit.

When the judge barked out the decree of "four months in the pen," I felt myself sink further down the wooden bench questioning to myself *'How could she keep fucking up like this?!'*

Grandpa, old, gray, and frail sat beside me squeezing my hand, lowering his Latino head in pain. He had seen too many of his children in and out of prison, or rehab, and even one shot down by the Detroit police a year after I was born. Grandma had passed just a few years back, his life filled now with too much heartache. I held my anger back, leaned my head onto his shoulder, he reached over squeezing me tight. We said nothing.

Single Parent

Mom and Dad's split happened in the summer of '85. Me and
six year old Carrie pranced around in our pink and blue Care
Bear nightgowns poking Barbie and Ken in and out of their
Dream House. Ken's van packed with all their friends, Barbie's
Corvette hitched to the van for private getaways on the
camping trip.

Carrie, straight haired with big dimple holed cheeks was all the
opposite of my fair-skinned, curly head, outgoing personality.
Mom called her, her little brown turd when she was born,
always the crybaby, hard to please. When it came to me, Mom
just said I was easy, ate, slept, shit and grinned.

Breakfast smells of chorizo and eggs filtered up the stairs that
day. My stomach growled, but interrupted by a maddening roar
bringing both Carrie and I trembling to our feet. Curiosity
forced us down the stairs. Carrie in fear, and face filled of tears,
held the backs of my arms, but her trust in me kept her moving
on. Mom's pounding presence echoed in the small hallway next
to the stairwell. Now at its edge I peeked around the corner,
Dad stood in his familiar fatigues, ragged jeans, tie-dye T,
leather vest to finesse, topped off with his battered leather hat
hiding his brown curls, and without shoes to end. He escaped
one smack to the head only to collide with another. She pushed
his shoulders with her fists forcing his backward stance in
motion toward us. Dad was nearer to us now. Glimpses caught
of Mom's five foot body came between shoves. Her dark hair
flailing, it stuck into the crooks of her mouth coming out in spits
of profanities. I never saw her so angry, started listening to her
furious words. "Where's the money!...fuck you!...piece of
shit!...what did you do!...hate!....good for nothing!"

Our trembling eyes shot tears from Dad's face. He gave in, and sprinted out the back door. Mom quickly locked it, giving one last spout to the closed door, noticed us, and snarled "Get back upstairs!" We didn't listen, dodging to the back window instead, crying and pleading for her to let Daddy back in. He stood in the backyard crying to the door. Mom backed away, returning with an object, opened the door, lashing what I saw now to be a not so small ceramic vase at his head. Blood spewed, he fell to his feet, crumpled, and back into a seizure on the cement ground. We thought he was dying.

I first experienced loss of a cherished life the summer before. A pit-bull invaded our backyard, tore my cat Cookie apart in our garage. I was the one who found her that morning. If Cookie hadn't made it in for the night she'd hang out in the garage. The door was broken, hung off its rusty hinges, making it easy for her to get in and out. I woke up to let her in, she didn't come when I called, I walked out the back door and saw the large black evil bull, ran back in before it caught me in its gaze. I knew what that dog did.

The minutes watching Dad's quaking body felt like hours, but then an unkempt man in jean shorts leapt over our metal fence to his aid, saving him. Dad didn't share Cookie's fate that day, but Mom just drew the blinds on him. Soon after the ambulance sirens came, a knock from a man with a badge in blue, she left it unanswered.

Sounds of BillyJoe waking now clear from Mom's bedroom. Only three years old, not walking, not talking, and still in a baby's crib. She immediately answered his cry, gently closing the bedroom door behind her, leaving us to stay hidden in our room.

I don't remember how long we stayed secluded in the house that day, but Dad never returned to live with us again. They separated, the divorce made it final in '87, and I turned nine years old.

I hated that he had gone. Mom made me say bad things to him once when he called "Don't call here...I don't want to talk to you." I said. My stomach ached after those words came out, it didn't feel right, and I know I hadn't meant what I said, Mom was using me.

Dad and Mick

We didn't see much of Dad again until the summer of '88, spending sparse nights at Grandma Phoebe's in the make shift basement apartment Dad lived in. Scary stories lifted from Stephen King novels made real to us. The cursing hand of the gypsy man living nearby in the woods, the devil is nearby when a crow is in sight. I was scared but also curious. Carrie's pipes always busted out tears. BillyJoe bewildered with smiles crawled up Dad's legs so he could be near. I never liked when it was time to go back home to Mom again, always left wondering why Dad wouldn't take us in.

He wasn't there to share the first few years of my life either, a distraught day in '77 took him away. My father was a gambler, and not a bad one. We were at the race track. A new family, I formed the bulge under my Mother's stretched tummy skin. The day cut short due to upsets of beer drunken non-winnings, she roared time to go, there was an accident. The kid drove a Ford Pinto. The minor hit igniting the car's gas tank in front of us into flames. We were fine, the young man wasn't, and Dad went away for two years.

Winter came. Dad got his own place so we could come and stay over the weekends. It was a small trailer home in Brownstown off Telegraph Road, a bit battered but didn't matter to me. It came with a bedroom for the three of us to share, opposing Dad's room, split by the open kitchen and living room off its alley-way shape. We'd play cards, eat pizza, and dance around with Dad to Jagger singing "Jumpin' Jack Flash is a gas gas gas" and end the night teary eyed to Mick telling us "You can't always get what you want." This song tugged at my Dad's heart, I saw his tears, made me cry too.

Dad's soul was torn by memories from his time as a combat medic in Vietnam. Nothing could have prepared his eyes for the trauma he saw, it would endure forever for him.

Veteran hospitals couldn't mend his heart. Haunted thoughts of fallen brothers he couldn't save sedated by needles filled with Heroine's liquid paradise. A habit ceased as doctors packed him full with bottles of promised hope to silence his pains.

I wished he could be around more often, just eleven now, but I understood why the pain inside kept him away.

Funeral Fumes

A planned weekend getaway at Dad's place spoiled by a phone call one freezing Saturday morning. The date, January 14th 1989. Our packed bags sat by the door, I was dressed and ready to go. No more jokes and scares, no more music romps, no more weekends spent with Dad.

Shame crept up my spine on reaching the doors of The Harry J. Will Funeral Home. We were running late. Mom's drinking began hours before the wake, and she carried it on with a small blue thermos cocktail mix of vodka and grapefruit juice. She swayed seated at the front bench. She was doused in cheap ladies perfume, dressed in a mid-thigh tight black skirt with a cleavage revealing top, bottomed off with black heels a little too high for this event.

Me, Joe, and Carrie, sat on the floor nearby. My eyes fixated on Mom seated alone, teary eyed, squinting, smashing her lips tightly together. She took another sip, gripping the thermos tightly with white-knuckeled hands. Unchanged eyes gazed on Dad's body lying in his casket. I wondered what was on her mind.

The funeral doors let out a bang just then, silencing the muffled sounds of conversations from people dressed in dark. It was Johnny, not at all dressed respectfully for the occasion. He strutted down the aisle outfitted in his trash man work attire, blackened hands and face, filth-filled Carhartt jumpsuit. My face burned sun red, glowing.

Mom and Johnny's introduction was made way by her friendship with one of his sisters. He came from a family of near a dozen siblings! Lived out in Taylor and now resided with us.

He seemed nice, was polite, but I still wasn't sure if I liked him, didn't know too much of him, just his age of twenty-nine, a few years younger than Mom, small guy, had some kind of southern mixed twang to his speech, and curly brown fro hair.

BillyJoe hopped into the casket with Dad to lie down, didn't understand why Mom pulled at him to get out or why Dad wouldn't wake up. He fell to the floor in a fit of tears and rage causing the people around to back away. It was time for us to go.

A subtle violence loomed beneath the air on the ride home in Johnny's rust blue van. The radio rattled whispered screams from its bare boned interior 'Pho...to...graph....I don't want your...pho...to...graph. I wanna touch ya!' Mom's eyes on the rolling scenery through the passenger window. Me and Carrie sat side by side on the dim carpet floor capsule in the back of the van. BillyJoe now quiet, rested on the floor sucking a baby bottle of juice, twiddling his brown baby waves between his pointer finger and thumb. Five years old, still in diapers, still no words, and still demanding the bottle.

Johnny silently smoked keeping his eyes on the road. Mom slobbered something. I only made out the end "hrmmph" and the evil glare to Johnny as we slowed up to halt at the corner stop sign across from our house. Mom unleashed herself from the van in a mad bolt run, hysteric and crying through the metal gates enclosing our backyard. I thought it strange she couldn't wait another minute to get out.

Funeral day, my alarm went off at 7:00 a.m, it was scheduled for noon. I woke up to Mom sprawled out on the kitchen floor stinking of the piss and booze puddle in which she was lying, snoring a deep sleep, oblivious. Our arrival would be late again.

We made it in time for the car march to the cemetery. Eric our older brother, but divided by fathers, had towhead painted pale skin and just turned sixteen. He would drive us in our busted-rusted up banana boat station wagon Mom just bought for $500 bucks. The funeral guy ran up, attaching four flags to the top of our car, it was the end of the line for us.

Mom's tales of us being oustcasts from Dad's side of the family became truth to me that day. Sidelong looks, upturned noses, all confirmed Mom's stories. They had never thought Mom or us good enough.

I didn't really care, I felt the need to become stronger for BillyJoe and Carrie's sake. They were younger, Carrie would begin to understand, but BillyJoe never would.

Rigid Routine

Now at twenty-two and twenty-one me and Carrie were back home taking over what was once ours and now Mom's sleeping quarters during her stay at the Hamtramck Women's facility in 2000. It was like we were girls again, minus the Barbies. Sharing a bed as we always did, scattered clothes and shoes covering the floor, and now fighting over the mirror for primping. It felt good to be home. Odd, but I always had a feeling of safeness here.

I bailed out on my 9 to 5 down the road to be at home with BillyJoe. It was a dead end paper pusher job anyway, the owner a prissy pushy man bitch, I was glad that I had an excuse to let it go. Taking care of Joe was a fulltime gig, had to be available twenty-four seven. Carrie stayed on waitressing, tending bar at the pub off Oak Street, the immediate extra cash was much needed. BillyJoe's check didn't come until the first of the month, by the end sometimes we ran short.

BillyJoe stuck to the rigidity of his routine Monday through Friday, but was a little more willing to compromise with us on weekends. In the morning around 7:00 a.m., about the same time I'd have to wake up and pee, he'd be there lying naked in the tub, looking at me saying "Heee!" meaning 'Clean me Sissy.'

His man growth started at about thirteen. The hair running down his legs grown thicker, mustache starting to surface, light patches of a beard wanting to come in, chest bare but for a few hairs growing around his nipples. A streak of watery shit ran down the tub from under his ass to the larger clump sitting in the drain, and as with every morning BillyJoe greeted me with his a.m. bone, a phenomenon that teenage *boys* only deal with, but first introduced to *me* by BillyJoe years ago.

I yanked the shower curtain closed so I could have an inkling of pee privacy. Questioning him as I always did, "Why won't you shit in the toilet!?" sometimes I would even show him mine drifting in the toilet bowl water pointing to my butt then to the toilet yelling "This is where it goes," then flush it down. He'd just look at me gritting his teeth giving a punch to the tile wall saying "HMM….HEY!" meaning 'start the fucking water Sissy!!' I always complied, turning the water on, only filling it half way to scrub all the shit away from his ass coloring the water brown, make him stand until it all rinsed down the drain. Now I could add clear waters and soap to a clean rag to scrub him down.

Clean, I let him sit in the tub for a minute while he giggled, swaying his big body in the tub, soaking the floor. "Let the water out Joe!" I yelled to him, so he would get out. Wouldn't dry off, stood there holding a towel against his body dripping wet, waiting for *me* to dry him. Next step, retrieving his attire for the day from his broken dresser drawers in Mom's bedroom, toss 'em on the toilet tank, dry his big ass down, then order him to take his clothes in the living room where he would wait to be dressed.

BillyJoe slipped his naked butt under the throw blanket on the living room couch. I grabbed his plastic tray of meds from the kitchen cupboard. He had been taking most of the five different meds since he was twelve years old, don't know how much they really helped, he still had his outbursts, still obsessed over taking baths and going for car rides, self-abuse, and destruction against the house, all the same. The seizure medication seemed to help though, stopped them from happening as often, but never ceased.

He never fought it, took the pills with gulps of water down in between. Joe mostly refused to dress himself, this time I won. He put on his underwear, socks, BUM sweatshirt, jeans, and high top shoes, he left the lace tying to me. He'd kick his leg up on my thigh for me to do it. The bus came, Joe knew the sound, wouldn't ever leave without his backpack full of his favorite snacks of barbeque chips, peanut butter crackers, and Faygo Cola. I tossed his bag to him then he blew through the front door running onto the school bus, always buckling up in the same seat.

Just because BillyJoe was without understanding didn't mean we were soft on him, wouldn't be right if his older sisters couldn't pick on him. Back home from school one night, and not ready to give him a bath yet, I decided to ban him from the tub.

BillyJoe always high tailed it from the bus to the bathroom for a dip in the tub after school. One time I ran, blocking him out of the bathroom, pushing him into the back bedroom, and locked him out. He yelled "HAAAAA!" pounding and twisting the knob. Carrie heard what was going on, and joined in. We knocked at the door asking "Who is it?" He pounded harder and louder turning the knob with more force. He knew he wasn't getting anywhere, wisen'd up and went out the back door running. Laughing, I opened the backdoor to a pile of clothes he had been wearing, we started laughing even harder running out the door, faced with BillyJoe's nakedness barreling through the back gate and heading to the front door to get in.

There was no stopping him, the neighborhood getting a quick flash of naked Joe in the snow. Good thing he was running and no cars were passing by, just the usual neighbors. But that didn't stop someone from calling the cops that day, many didn't like us, and they didn't understand, didn't want to.

Homecoming

Four months later it was pick-up day. Carrie road shotgun in our beat-up Toyota Camri, never any help with direction, and BillyJoe never cared where we were headed, just sat back enjoying the long ride, eyes gazing over the ever changing landscape. Always knew when we were in Detroit city limits, pot-holed streets and board up windows, lawns overgrown and empty houses, more liquor stores loitered by hoes and bums than you ever saw anywhere else, and a weighted ugliness everywhere. We drove deep into the city from the west side to east, destination Hamtramck, my first time there, the neighborhood no better than Detroit itself, the area seemed worse to me, more homes abandoned, burned out, or just burnt to the ground. At least the weather was beautiful, bright and sunny in May of 2000, a great day to be released from prison Mom would have to agree.

We never visited her during her four month stint in the clink. Heard from her by mail, letters full of sweetness ending in 'xo xo xo' sending kisses to her 'baby boy BillyJoe.' Daily collect calls filled with demands and questions on how we were caring for him, "Did you give Joe a ride today?" "You know he has to go!" "How are you bathing him?" "Did you shave him?" "He needs a haircut!" always ending her calls in conversations with BillyJoe. He'd listen to her voice, sometimes say "Ha" prop the phone on his shoulder for a bit, hang up on her when he was done listening.

Mom was released and put into a half-way house the night before to be evaluated. There was no sign to identify the place from its neighboring residential homes, crumbling brick, windows dark with dust, white paint peeling from its door, didn't make sense how this place could help reform. Mom shot out the door just as we pulled up, she must have been watching for us. Joe saw her, quickly unbuckled himself from the backseat ejecting from the car before I could come to a complete stop. As I caught sight of her the weight on my shoulders lifted, relieved to have her back home.

Mom's gray wings spread further down from her temples, couldn't dye it during her stay, her skin hardened, lighter, and older. BillyJoe grabbed a tight hold around Mom's elbow sayin' "Ma...Ma!" in a grunting voice. Forcefully guiding her down the busted steep cement stairs and into the backseat of the car to sit with him. I peered back at them through the rearview mirror smiling with a slight teary giggle. Her speech thickened with improper word pronunciation, overflowing with street slang, didn't sound right coming from her forty-four year old face. "That's not how you talk." I said. She snapped back "Donts starts with me ingrate!" and went back on to talking with BillyJoe. I wasn't in the mood to argue with her, bit my tongue, not mentioning her lack of gratitude for keeping things up behind her mess.

We headed back through Detroit stopping down on Trumbull Street for a first meet with her probation officer and the fitting of an electric house arrest ankle bracelet, the tether a condition of her early release. Six months of house arrest with two years more of probation followed her four month jail sentence, but it beat staying in. Seemed like a do-able task, because why would you fuck it up when you know the consequence is getting your ass locked back up!?

I remember Carrie and I spent a weekend in jail for drinking under age in '96. A first and last for me. A fight had broke out in front of our friend's house is how we got caught. Mom didn't have the cash to bail us out, not sure she cared to anyway, so we had to wait for the judge until Monday. It wasn't full blown prison, but still a human cage, I never wanted to relive that experience, never late, never missed a payment on my probation dues, I was done, and never got caught again.

Mom went up alone, hoped it wouldn't take her very long, the air conditioning system conked out a few weeks back, it was getting later in the afternoon with temps rising, I worried BillyJoe would get overheated, and his face had already gone into a bit of a panic, worried that Mom wouldn't return again. "She'll be back, you have to wait." I said. He responded with gritting teeth and a punch to the seat.

We lined up our car with the other battered vehicles awaiting their beloved criminal husbands, boyfriends, girlfriends, children, or wives of all colors, connected only by vice and poverty, each reporting to their respective probation officers. Babies crying, kids screaming, adults yelling at each other or the kids, or to someone on their cell phones, I was getting sick of the same old scene, angry because I didn't know how to get out, or because I didn't know who to turn to.

Her probation officer bought her story for having to run errands for BillyJoe, allowing us to go for an early dinner at Mexican Gardens out in Taylor. Couldn't hit Mexican town in Detroit because they didn't carry items on the menu BillyJoe demanded, but Mexican Gardens served one of his favorite dishes, fried shrimp!

It was always tough to sit down in a restaurant with Joe, he just didn't have the patience for it, or desire to be in a room packed full of strangers and their loud noises. He surprised me this time, followed the waitress to our designated booth, sitting down without being told, face beaming with joy as Mom sat down next to him. BillyJoe laughing at us uncontrollably triggered our own giggles. It was a good day.

I hoped this was the start of new beginnings, hoped the system finally came through on reforming her, hoped she finally got over his death.

Trash Man

Johnny's final day on this earth was set to the rising sun one early summer's morning in '99. He was on his way to work in his prized sky blue GEO Tracker. Piece of shit, it was precious to him, his first new car. No longer drove like it once did though, wild rage romps with Mom left the vehicle scarred with key marks from side to side, soft black top torn from a steak knife's blade Mom used to settle a score, and over-packed with miles from long drives with BillyJoe. A seasoned trash man at the age of Thirty-nine, on the job over a decade now, he hit Pennsylvania road at 5:45 a.m., the semi hit him at the intersection coming off Allen road at 5:54 a.m. The driver didn't stop when the light turned red. We were told Johnny died on impact, told it was instant. His body was thrown from the car they said, the top must have been down, seatbelt unbuckled. I nearly shed a tear when the call came with the news.

Many of my memories involve Johnny being half naked, dancing, and high. He liked prancing around in his underwear. Johnny's black Calvin Klein jockeys with tube socks up to his knees was one of his most legendary attires. Dancing across the open kitchen room floor, hands rubbing down his thin muscular hairy chest, smoking, singing to the air, "And I want...and I need...and I love... ANIMAL!" Head filled delusions of illustriousness leading him to believe he was God's gift to pussy, his obsessive vanity was strange to me, I had never seen a grown man act in such a way, but he wasn't mean and tended to do what Mom said. Always there to pick us up from school, made breakfast omelets, and often helped out with BillyJoe.

The steps for a lawsuit over Johnny's death were taken quickly. I thought the money awarded to her would be good, would help out in paying off debt, getting things together, in order, taking care of BillyJoe, for maybe even the rest of his life and hers combined. I don't know how she let it all turn so wrong.

Rerun

Her homecoming from prison allowed for some relief in my life. She was there to take charge of BillyJoe again. I could take off for the night, just had to be back by ten in the morning to take her orders. If it wasn't probation, AA, meds, or doctor appointments for Joe, it was groceries, driving, and trips to the bank to unload some cash.

I never questioned the amounts withdrawn, just did as I was instructed, never wanted a fight over it. The drive thru bank teller's questioning expression revealed what was on her mind as she would slide the dough into the mechanical metal drop door. 'Back again...what the hell are you doing with all this money!?' I'm sure she thought I was a druggie or thief, or something. But I didn't look back, grabbed the money, buckled up, and sped on taking a quick glance at Joe sitting content in the backseat before speeding out of the drive. Mom wanted me to drop off the money before taking Joe for a ride.

We hit the red light at Pennsylvania and Quarry roads where the 76 gas station, Dairy-Mart, and Village Green apartments sat. Victor's liquor store a bit of the way down on Quarry was our view at the intersection. I thought the child proof locks in my Saturn Sedan were set, but I was mistaken when Joe pulled up the lock making a wild dash across the street toward Victor's store. Time seemed to stop in his quest because the car turning left in his direction missed his steps. Fear stopped my heart, but not my reflexes. I slammed on the gas pedal squealing into the gas station running from the car after BillyJoe into the liquor store.

Joe's shopping already complete and him heading for the door as I entered gasping for my breath and furious. Victor, an overfriendly dark hairy middle-eastern man never minded what Joe took, just rang it up and entered it in on our ongoing tab. I grumbled through my teeth as we walked down the street back to the car "Dammit Joe...don't fuckin' do that shit!" He wasn't listening to me.

One eye constant on BillyJoe through my rearview mirror, his eyes on the rolling scenery, crunching bites of Cabana barbeque chips washed down by gulps of a Faygo cola. Left at 15th street, another down to St. Ignace past the little mouthy hag's house yelling "Whore!" to me from her front porch, the wave of my middle finger in return. It was one of our delightful daily exchanges.

I had become a target of profane slander from a teeny teenage blonde girl with thanks to my ex Kevin who knocked her up some months ago. She had developed an obsessive jealously of me. I must have been the source of one of their many violent disputes just before. Now past 16th, relieved to be back at home. BillyJoe blasted through the gates before me, hands already pulling at his belt to undress for another soak in the tub, his fourth of the day.

The house darker these days, Johnny dead about a year, summer again, no more torn up cars, shattered windows, butchered and burned skins, no more drama to occupy her. The blinds clipped tight, a cloud of smoke held steady throughout. She no longer cleaned like she use to, scattered beer cans on the table and kitchen counters, dishes piled high and dirty in the sink, stove stained with old food, and scattered litter from the everydays all over. My friends now hers, finding kinship in their vice, all familiar faces surrounding the kitchen table.

Staci's twiggy stick figure ripped past me, hiding her face, lighting up a cigarette and out the back door, odd she didn't say anything to me as she passed. The smoke blocked his face but nothing could block Kevin's loud mouth, Mom giggled, no wonder why that bitch was running her mouth again across the street. Kevin smiled at me, I rolled my eyes threw the cash down on the table in front of Mom's place, she snatched it, tucking it in her bra. "He's in the tub again, I washed him earlier." I said "I knows how to takes care of my baby-boy, you donts tell me!" She barked. I walked away to join Staci out back.

Staci stood facing the gate puffing away, swaying side to side. I took a seat in the chipped away white stained wooden chair sitting in the open sun, lit up a Newport taking a long drag and asked "What's your deal?" A delayed then broken Staci spoke "My.....si...nusessss...." "Sounds like more than that, you're not speaking right." I asked looking at her puzzled. "I.....too...k.....one.....of......your Mom's... pill... is... I... got....ta....blow......my nose." She fast stepped back into the house slamming the screen door behind her. I didn't believe her, she lied a lot to people, including me, never really understood why she tried to hide who she was. Maybe she didn't know herself, not sure if anyone ever did.

I sunk down into my seat dazing into the sun. I was getting tired of this scene, all these people running in and out, drunk and high, some my friends, some not, always a party, or a another celebration about nothing, coming over, being around, staying nights when I wasn't even there. I mostly stayed in BillyJoe's room these days, always too many bodies filling up the place.

The sound of the screen door opening hit the back of my ears.
Keys jiggled "Sissy." BillyJoe said dropping the car keys in my
lap. It was time to go again. I was glad, I needed a ride too.
I had stopped my drug use the summer before, stuck to booze,
easier to control, could always puke it out.

Spin

Luckily she was home when he dropped me off. I tumbled from Dennis' black Jeep Cherokee at 2:00 a.m., laughing, floating on the cool summer air. My body tingled all over. I had only taken half a hit of **E**, but made a judgment error on blending in the vodka and pot. My hair damp, fuzzed out from our Jacuzzi dip with strangers, I couldn't tell you where that place even was, only that it was down deep in Detroit, had only known Dennis the spinnin' druggie DJ for maybe three weeks, I hooked up with him in a club one night, dumb move to say the least.

He sped off after I got up stumbling to the fence, struggling then finally making my way into the backyard. The door was locked so I pounded for someone to let me in. "Dammit!" Mom yelled in response. "Just let me in," I whispered to the door. Mom welcomed me with a scowling face. I gave her a kiss and glided by. "The bitch is fuckin' high," she said slamming the door shut. I didn't feel in line with the floor so I used the wall for assistance on my path to the kitchen to raid the fridge, hoping food would get rid of the spin in my head.

My ears throbbed, I could hardly hear her, caught the words "What...drug....on...fuck" from her as she stood against the stove watching me pull the jar of cheese dip from the fridge and corn chips off the top, slamming myself and dinner down at the kitchen table. My hand couldn't find my mouth as I tried feeding myself. I thought by now some of my buzz should have slowed, the food wasn't working and my body felt compressed, the sound of my heart overpowering. I got scared, knew I had to get some of this shit out of my system. I ran to the bathroom ramming my fingers down my throat, white foamy shit was all I could get up, 'Had I ate today?' I wondered. Mom yelled and yelped. The phone rang. It was that shit who just dropped me off. "What the fuck did you give my daughter!?" she blasted at him over the phone, ending her tirade with threats to get his ass arrested if she ever caught him around our house or me again.

I got up what I could, the trails slowed and the pressure from my ears faded, I could sleep now. I curled up on the bathroom rug, the cool floor beneath made me feel better. Mom came in, threw a towel over me, she got up throughout the night flicking the lights on and off, nudging me to make sure I was still breathing. I was done with drugs.

Parlor Dancer

It was about one o' clock in the afternoon when I walked in. Outside the hot sun shimmered. Inside the house it was dark, blinds drawn, the central air blew low. The radio played some techno dance tune. BillyJoe was in school. I spied Mom dancing alone in the living room, a pint of Jack Daniels on the table next to an iced glass half filled of whiskey. She didn't notice me, the music was too loud. I just stood back watching her for a few minutes.

Mom moved around the room doing her mix of aerobic slash exotic dancer moves, making faces, pumping her arms up in the air, bouncing from side to side, feeling down her thighs, the works. My laugh gave me away. Mom stopped, and the anger flooded in. She quick stepped to the kitchen taking her seat at the table next to her drink. Her heavy breathing started, I knew what was to come, tried to ignore it by raiding the fridge, retrieving some left over spaghetti in a small plastic container, nuking it in the microwave to be fast. I grabbed a fork taking a seat across from her asking "Do you need anything today?" thinking this would help subdue the anger. No response, the microwave timer went off. She grumbled. "Yous thinks your better than mes?" "I just asked a question" I said. "Thinks yous knows somethin!" she said. Her eyes now filling with tears, "I had a goods life, we were good, then you ruined it!" "What are you talking about!?" I questioned. "You knows bitch! Yous wanted him, always takes from mes!" I boiled. I knew what she implied. "Fuck you!!!" I screamed. She threw her drink in my face, I reacted fast, quickly flipping the table up at her, but not high enough to make it flip, or knock the Jack down. I ran grabbing my keys off the counter, but her reaction came too fast, yanking my hair in pony tail from the back, pulling me into her arms, she was after my car keys, we wrestled a minute, I wasn't as strong as her. I ran out the front door to the neighbors, calling the cops. It was the only way I would get my keys back. She heard the sirens and threw the keys out the front window to the pavement.

My traveling closet, my car trunk, the possibility of being thrown out or items destroyed by her was always there. Now where would I stay? I had quit my job eight months before to take care of BillyJoe so I didn't have any money. I had a new boyfriend, dating just six months, I was afraid to ask. Would he let me stay?

As I drove, I cried. *How did she twist the past into an affair?*

Singled Out

I had made one of my first drunken slumber mistakes at seventeen years old in the summer of '95. Surprising? No. Not the first time a man many years beyond mine tried grasping at my youth, just thought me and Johnny were cool. Suppose that's why I felt more betrayed then violated when I awoke to his unwanted hand gesture beneath my covers.

My mistake, I chose to pass out on the floor of Eric's vacated bedroom. The room had stayed empty long since his move. BillyJoe didn't want to take it over, preferred sleeping downstairs, and really wouldn't come up here since the fire.

I pulled out an old blanket stuffed in the closet, grabbed some dirty pajamas laying on the ground by my bedroom door, rolled up in the blanket, and crashed out on the carpeted floor.

The fear woke me sober. His hand still stuck in my panties, he lay next to me pretending to be asleep. I didn't want to believe it. It was dark but I recognized his smell and could make out the shape of his body, I rolled away releasing his hands from my pants, dropped the fear and got angry, I started kicking him in his head, telling him to "Get the fuck out of here!" He ran downstairs quickly, silently. I came down to Mom's room crying at her side, trying to get out what had happened.

Her reaction calm, too calm, gently telling him to leave. Did she not understand what had happened!? I grabbed my purse and car keys heading for the back door, Mom blocked my way, I ran to the front, Johnny stood guard crying at my threats of heading to the police station "I am sorry, it won't happen again, I didn't know what I was doing!" Mom came in behind backing his whine up, "Lisa, BillyJoe is on his insurance, his medication, . . . you can't." I gave in, Johnny left. I slept.

That night I learned there was truth in what my twelve year old friend Karen had told me about Johnny one pajama party night back in sixth grade, a story and accusation about Johnny that had put him away for eighteen months. Mom knew the story, and the rumors around of another possible molestation. It taught me that there was truth in what Staci told me about how he was acting before he dropped her off at her house. I learned that jail can't turn off what turns someone on. A creep is a creep, without redemption.

Mom let him return a week after the incident, the story was that, oh yeah, he was high, didn't know what he was doing see, the mescaline was to blame. Bullshit.

A Ms. Keller showed up at my school right around this time, a petite older black woman dressed in all gray. The principal's aid called me out of my English class to meet with her. At first I thought maybe she knew I had been drinking.

On entering the room with Ms. Keller, she greeted me sweetly, asking, "How are you doing today?" My guard was up, it was an odd encounter, I coldly replied "Fine." Sitting down in a desk far from her, she asked if I knew why she was here, I shook my head unknowingly, and she began a story that was told to her agency by an unnamed relative concerned for the children's welfare in my home. I blasted back at her in furious denial of the allegations. "I am almost eighteen and there ain't nothing you can do or take away from me!" I ran from the classroom, down the hall, blasting my way through the double metal glass doors, high speed down the one block it took to get back home and locked myself in my room, reaching for comfort in a fifth of Absolute I kept secreted away in my closet.

I was the mangy dog digging for scraps of love on the outskirts of our house, 'why did she choose him over me?' I thought, I was her daughter, she didn't care what happened to me, enjoyed that I hurt, wanted me to have heartache like she did, wanted me to never succeed, wanted to keep me down, didn't want me to have a better chance in life. Mom.

Bathing Dreams

The heat was unmerciful that steamy day in June of '02. I was out in desperate search for an affordable air conditioning unit for my shabby-chic little apartment in Royal Oak. I walked in the door hearing Carrie's voice telling me "Pick up the phone," then hanging up, the answering machine was lit with fifteen of the same messages, the phone rang again, her at the other end, all she said was, "Joe is dead." I screeched back, hurtling the phone at the wall, nearly breaking it in two. Joe was only nineteen years old when he passed, a seizure took hold, held him under water in his favorite getaway, the bathtub.

I had moved in with my new man, a different sort for me. We were in a quaint little one-bedroom apartment miles away, and I was trying at a different kind of life. Mom and Carrie had moved to New Boston with Joe the winter before. The place was secluded, sitting on a half acre lot, twice the size of our house in Wyandotte. The master bedroom had its own bathroom with an oversize Jacuzzi-style bathtub that quickly became Joe's favorite place. I never thought it would be his coffin.

The new house would give her some peace I thought, maybe change her ways. The drive was far for the drunks and druggies that hung out at the old place so most stopped coming around, and she still had to wear the tether. But she fucked it up, ending up back in the slammer again.

It was about 3:00 a.m. when the phone rang, it was Carrie who told me, the cops came and took Mom away, Uncle Rick had been there and they had got into a fight. Mom bashed him in the head with something Carrie said. Mom was the one who actually called the police, but when they arrived and saw that

black plastic ankle bracelet she was wearing, they took her in.
They weren't letting her back out, no bail, and now she had to
do all her time behind bars. One year in prison making out the
Power of Attorney to leave Carrie at the helm.

My obligations stripped a year ago. Mom accused me of
stealing and I moved away. I later found out Carrie was the one
who put that rumor in her head. I never confronted the false
claim. For once in her life she apparently wanted to take charge
of Mom's ordeals, so I decided to let it go. At first it allowed for
me to finally start working on myself. I was twenty-four now. I
got a good job at a big corporation, began classes at the local
community college, things going well in the new relationship,
and a future worth looking forward to. Then the calls started.

I don't know what was happening over there, I don't know what
she was doing. BillyJoe's violent outbursts became more and
more frequent by her account. He was punching holes in the
walls, throwing tantrums, rage fits, and having more seizure
attacks than usual.

Whenever I visited the house, it was always a mess, clothes
spilled out over the floor, dishes in the sink, empty beer and
liquor bottles overflowing from large trash bags hanging on
doorknobs, and it smelled. Strange to me because Carrie always
liked things tidy, sparkly clean, bleached and smelling sweet. I
on the other hand, always pushed those chores off till the very
end, but then again she was a new Mom.

Carrie had popped out another baby six months before, and this
one she had decided to keep. She had let the father, a new
boyfriend, move in, as well as a part of his family to help out. I

still don't know if any one of them had jobs. They were always just there it seemed.

BillyJoe's health problems escalated, he was getting worse. Shortly after he turned eighteen he couldn't go to the DMC *Children's* Hospital, and I couldn't get any one on staff there to give me a referral for a doctor who could treat a now adult with an autism like his. The doctor that Mom found for him didn't seem to know how to handle his case, just ran his blood work and kept filling the same scripts he'd been on since he was twelve. Joe was crumbling, he missed his Mom I thought. I made calls and trips to get help, sent documents to Carrie that went unattended, unnoticed, or just left untouched.

I found out about the cash when arranging for his funeral, it was nearly gone! Only $20,000 left from hundreds of thousands! When I demanded to know what happened to it all, Carrie blamed Mom's collect calls, but I knew better.

After the funeral I decided not to turn back. I moved, changed my number, didn't want to be found. My little brother was gone, his favorite past time now a permanent stay. I let go, let the old relationships die with him. I had to try living for me now.

END

Appendix

Lost words from my Father....

The worst of me
You've been with the worst of me
You say you still want me
Is that why the fear is there?

Prime
Young and in our prime
They swooped in just in time
So many cut-down in size

Calling
One visit came
Lifeless youthful calls maimed me from the wall
My brothers calling for my return

Present Past
Lost in a past where living was the only danger
I am never coming to the present

Vietnam Veteran and Father
~ William Joseph Kiel II

Better than Me

"So **you** think you're better than **me**?"

Echoes from her smoked stained glass

Image neared mirroring
Drinking from my flask

The past now distant, the pain still here

Am I better?

Developments made possible while out from your leer

I am sorry...but I must find a new path
Six years past since seeing you last

You will always be my Mother
And I love you alas

for Mom
~ Your oldest daughter

French Fry Fantasy

Burgers and fries would ever compromise

A Faygo, a fry, he'd never tell a lie
A touch not a must
His smile went for miles

He'd run
Then dance
Sometimes we'd prance

Head bunt round blasts
Mood shifts to feud
Sometimes I Boo-Hooed

Pop a med, take a cruise
Bathe again
Watch a toon, end the night with a snooze
Till the morn, to start once again

for BillyJoe
~ Sissy

Other Books from William Joseph K Publications

Available Today @ Amazon.com and Barnesandnoble.com

 *Episodes of the Norm* is an eclectic anthology of donated shorts, rants, slams, essays, and poems from various authors. Fifty percent of the proceeds are donated to the Autism Society of America! ISBN: 978-0-9820425-0-2

 *The Worm and The Caterpillar* children's book draws a comparison between the worm and the caterpillar who both begin life as crawling forms, but in the end wind up very different. It relates that the power of belief coupled with the will to try is an immeasurable force making any transformation possible. ISBN: 978-0-9820425-3-3

 *The Art of Boogie-Woogie* is a book of musical score. Now in its third edition, and coming with a companion CD, this book is a collection of forty-one bangin' left-hand base lines that will have you boogie'n like a pro! ISBN: 978-0-9820425-1-9

 *Blues Preludes* is a book of musical score. It is a collection of seven piano vignettes in complete score designed for the early learner. The book includes blues pieces intended to represent both a New Orleans and a Chicago blues sound and closes with a boogie woogie that will have your friends and fans tappin' along! ISBN: 978-0-9820425-2-6

www.williamjkpub.com